Searchlight
BOOKS™

What
Are Energy
Sources?

Finding Out about

Nuclear

Energy

Matt Doeden

Lerner Publications Company
Minneapolis

Lerner Publications Company
A division of Lerner Publishing Group, Inc.
241 First Avenue North
Minneapolis, MN 55401 USA

For reading levels and more information, look up this title at www.lernerbooks.com.

Library of Congress Cataloging-in-Publication Data

Doeden, Matt.
    Finding out about nuclear energy / by Matt Doeden.
        pages   cm. — (Searchlight books: What are energy sources?)
    Includes index.
    ISBN 978–1–4677–3655–8 (lib. bdg. : alk. paper)
    ISBN 978–1–4677–4640–3 (eBook)
    1. Nuclear energy—Juvenile literature. I. Title.
    TK9148.D64 2015
    621.48'3—dc23   2013039450

Manufactured in the United States of America
1 — BP — 7/15/14

Contents

Chapter 1

WHAT IS NUCLEAR ENERGY?

Imagine yourself on a beach. You hold a single grain of sand in your hand. It seems as though there's nothing to it, right? Wrong!

You can hold a lot of sand in your hand. What is a grain of sand made up of?

All matter is made up of atoms. Even a tiny grain of sand has about 60 quintillion atoms. That's 60 with eighteen zeros behind it! That should give you an idea of how small an atom is. Yet atoms hold huge amounts of energy.

Every atom in the universe contains energy. Imagine how much energy is on this beach!

Atoms are made up of three main parts. Protons and neutrons make up the center. It's called the nucleus. Electrons orbit the nucleus. The nucleus holds an atom's energy. Tapping into this gives us nuclear energy.

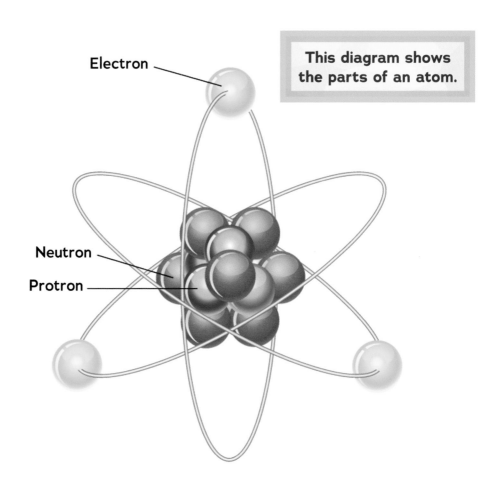

Electron

Neutron

Protron

This diagram shows the parts of an atom.

Fusion and Fission

There are two types of nuclear energy. They are fusion and fission. We combine two nuclei during fusion. This gives off a burst of energy. The sun is powered by fusion.

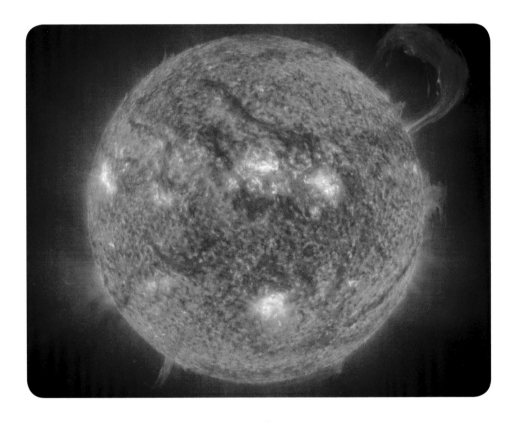

FUSION IN THE SUN GIVES OFF LARGE AMOUNTS OF LIGHT AND HEAT.

Fusion could provide almost limitless clean energy. There's just one problem. Scientists have to heat the fuel to very high temperatures. They don't know how else to make fusion happen. It takes more energy to make the atoms combine than we get out of it.

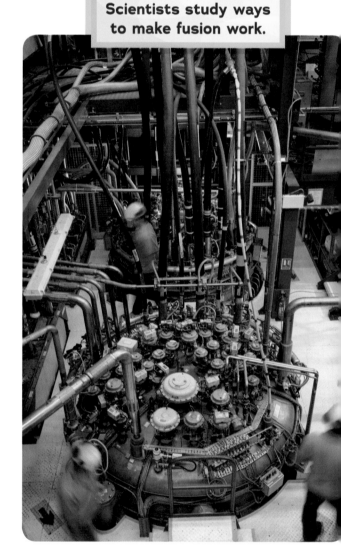

Scientists study ways to make fusion work.

That leaves us with fission. An atom's nucleus is split apart during fission. One atom splits into two smaller ones. And lots of energy is given off.

Uranium is an element often used in fission.

Fission is the type of energy that runs nuclear power plants. These plants provide about 11 percent of the world's electricity.

Nuclear power plants can be found around the world.

Chapter 2

PRODUCING NUCLEAR POWER

Not just any atoms will work in a power plant. Most times uranium atoms are used. Uranium can be found in nature, including in rocks and water.

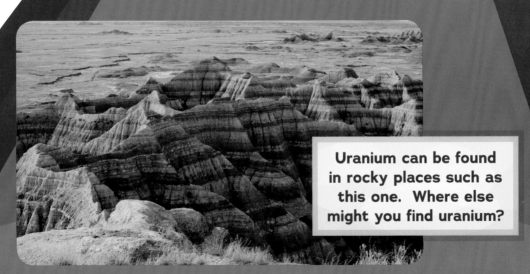

Uranium can be found in rocky places such as this one. Where else might you find uranium?

It Starts with Uranium

Uranium comes in several forms. The one used for nuclear power is uranium-235 (U-235). Less than 1 percent of all uranium on Earth is U-235. That doesn't sound like much. But think of it this way. About 2.2 pounds (1 kilogram) of U-235 can produce up to 3 million times more energy than 2.2 pounds of coal!

This illustration shows a U-235 atom.

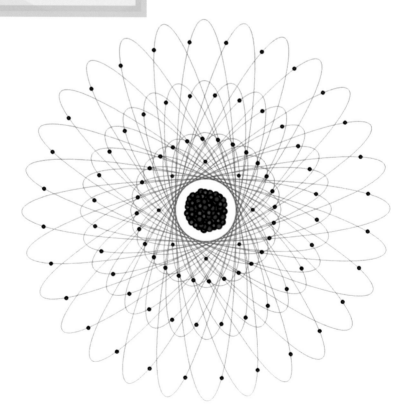

Uranium is found mixed with other rock and metals in ore. Ore is found all around the world. There are two main ways to mine ore. Open-pit mines are for ore close to Earth's surface. Large machines remove dirt and rock to get to the ore.

An open-pit mine is created by drilling and blasting Earth's surface.

Underground mines are for ore that is deep underground. Miners dig tunnels to get to the ore. The mined ore is then crushed. The uranium is separated from other rock and metal.

Miners dig tunnels to get at uranium deep underground.

We can also get uranium from water. Oceans and other bodies of water have uranium dissolved in them. We can separate this uranium from the water.

Dissolved uranium can be found in oceans.

Uranium found in nature doesn't have enough U-235 to be used in a power plant. The uranium must be changed. Workers make small pellets of uranium. The pellets are at least 3 percent U-235. That's enough to produce power.

Uranium pellets can produce a great amount of energy.

Inside the Reactor

The pellets go to a nuclear reactor in a power plant. A nuclear reactor is a complex machine. It controls the fission needed to produce electricity. There are a few types of these machines. But they all work in the same basic way.

A nuclear reactor generates energy from pellets of uranium.

It starts with the fuel. The pellets are placed inside metal rods. Each rod is about 14 feet (4 meters) long. The rods are placed in bundles.

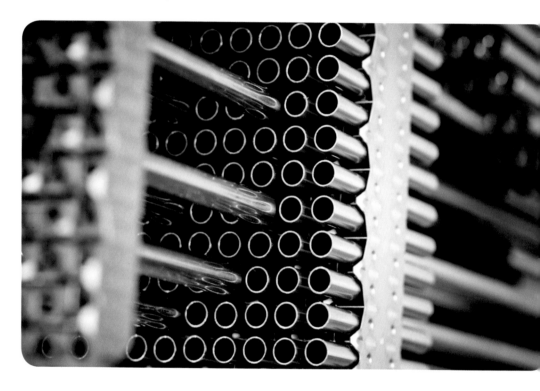

METAL RODS CONTAIN PELLETS OF URANIUM.

U-235 goes through radioactive decay. This means it naturally gives off energy and particles. These particles travel at very high speeds. The U-235 decays inside the metal rod. A particle hits another U-235 atom. That atom loses particles too. The particles keep hitting other atoms. They start a chain reaction.

While in the metal rods, the atoms give off energy.

Fuel rods are placed in the core of a nuclear reactor in Germany in 2010.

The chain reaction creates a lot of energy. This heats the metal rods. The rods are placed underwater. The heated rods turn the water into steam.

The moving steam spins the blades of a turbine.
The turbine drives a generator. This machine turns the
energy into electricity.

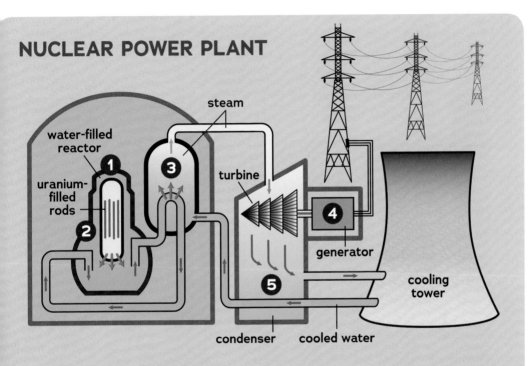

NUCLEAR POWER PLANT

steam

water-filled
reactor

uranium-
filled
rods

1

2

3

turbine

4

generator

5

condenser   cooled water

cooling
tower

1. Metal rods are filled with uranium pellets. The rods are placed
   in water in a nuclear reactor.
2. Uranium atoms split and release energy in the rods.
3. The energy heats water and creates steam.
4. The steam moves a turbine. The turbine turns a generator.
   This creates electricity.
5. The steam cools and turns into water. The water is used again
   in the process. A cooling tower may be used to release extra
   heat from the plant.

Workers can control how fast the chain reaction goes. But the reactors are very powerful. They are kept inside thick concrete walls. The plant has cooling systems. These keep the fuel from getting too hot.

Workers monitor the activity of the reactors.

Chapter 3

THE PROS AND CONS OF NUCLEAR POWER

All energy sources have pros and cons. Like fossil fuels, uranium is a nonrenewable resource. When the fuel is used up, it's gone forever. But we have enough uranium to last hundreds of years.

Uranium is a nonrenewable resource. What is another energy source that is nonrenewable?

Safety

Nuclear plants can produce lots of energy. But things can go wrong. And it can be a disaster. An explosion occurred at the Chernobyl plant in Ukraine in 1986. Huge amounts of radioactive materials were released. Radiation can cause cancer. Thousands have died from its effects.

One of the worst nuclear disasters in history occurred at the Chernobyl plant.

Such disasters are rare. Plants are safer than they were during Chernobyl's day. But nuclear disasters are not a thing of the past. An earthquake occurred near Japan in 2011. It caused several reactors there to fail. Explosions gave off deadly material. The disaster served as a reminder. Nuclear power is not completely safe.

A tsunami hit Japan in 2011. It caused several nuclear reactors to fail and to release deadly radiation.

Nuclear Waste

Nuclear fuel that has been used up is called spent fuel. Spent fuel can no longer start a chain reaction. But the fuel is still very radioactive. Even coming near a spent fuel rod can kill a person. And it remains deadly for thousands of years.

Spent fuel can be stored in deep pools.

Spent fuel has a very long life span, so it's important to store it safely and away from the public.

Governments around the world have searched for ways to get rid of spent fuel and other nuclear waste. Much of it is sealed in barrels and buried underground.

But some argue that even this isn't safe. Natural disasters could cause the barrels to leak. The waste could get into water supplies. That could be a disaster greater than any plant failure.

Some people worry nuclear waste could pollute water supplies.

Battling Climate Change

Still, nuclear power isn't all bad for the environment. Many people are worried about global climate change. Most of our energy comes from burning fossil fuels. But this puts huge amounts of carbon dioxide into the atmosphere.

Burning fossil fuels leads to air pollution, water pollution, and climate change.

Too much carbon dioxide in the atmosphere causes Earth to warm. And too much warming could cause disaster. Sea levels could rise. Changes in weather patterns could result in more severe droughts, floods, and fires.

CLIMATE CHANGE MIGHT INCREASE THE RISK OF WILDFIRES.

Nuclear power plants do not give off carbon dioxide. That means they do not contribute to climate change. In this way, nuclear power is good for the environment.

Nuclear plants give off steam, not smoke. Nuclear plants don't release carbon dioxide into the air.

Chapter 4

NUCLEAR POWER IN THE FUTURE

The use of nuclear power dropped after disasters at plants in the 1970s and the 1980s. Many people thought nuclear plants were too unsafe. People fought against new plants being built near their homes.

These people are protesting the use of nuclear power. Why might people not want a nuclear power plant near their homes?

Many people had changed their minds about nuclear power by the 2000s. New, safer plants were built around the world. And governments tightly control what is done with waste.

Workers build a nuclear plant in Tennessee in 2011.

People continue to search for alternative energy sources. Solar power, wind power, and hydropower are renewable. And they give off no or very little carbon dioxide.

These solar panels turn sunlight into electricity.

But they may not be enough to replace fossil fuels completely. That's why nuclear power is important. It could help supply the world's energy in the future.

Wind power is another renewable energy source.

The Dream of Cold Fusion

Imagine a world where we can get almost limitless power from seawater. There is no nuclear waste. That's the dream of cold fusion. Cold fusion is when we can get energy from combining atoms at room temperature. One of the likeliest ways this might happen is by combining the hydrogen atoms in seawater.

If cold fusion could be achieved, the world's oceans could provide almost limitless clean fuel.

For now, cold fusion is just a dream. Most scientists do not think it is possible. But some are still searching for ways to make it work. If we can figure it out, it could provide the world with huge amounts of clean energy. Will it ever happen? We don't know. But it's worth hoping.

SCIENTISTS CONTINUE TO WORK ON MAKING COLD FUSION A REALITY.

Glossary

alternative energy source: a source of energy other than traditional fossil fuels

atom: the smallest unit of an element that has the properties of the element. An atom is made up of protons, neutrons, and electrons.

chain reaction: a change to an atom that causes other atoms nearby to undergo change

electron: a part of an atom that orbits the nucleus and has a negative charge

fossil fuel: a fuel such as coal, natural gas, or oil that was formed over millions of years from the remains of dead plants and animals

neutron: a part of an atom that is located within the nucleus and has no charge

nonrenewable: not able to be replenished. Once a nonrenewable form of energy is gone, it is used up for good.

nucleus: the core of an atom, made up of protons and neutrons

proton: a part of an atom that is located within the nucleus and has a positive charge

radiation: the energy and particles that are given off by radioactive substances and nuclear reactions

radioactive: having or producing radiation

radioactive decay: the process by which certain atoms break down and release energy called radiation

renewable: able to be replenished over time

turbine: a machine with blades that converts the energy from a moving fluid or gas, such as steam, into mechanical energy

Learn More about Nuclear Energy

Books

Benoit, Peter. *Nuclear Meltdowns*. New York: Children's Press, 2012. Learn more about what happens when a nuclear reactor fails, or melts down, and read about famous meltdowns in history.

Doeden, Matt. *Finding Out about Coal, Oil, and Natural Gas*. Minneapolis: Lerner Publications, 2015. Fossil fuels remain our main source of energy. Learn more about how they form, how they're collected, and the pros and cons of using them.

Hansen, Amy S. *Nuclear Energy: Amazing Atoms*. New York: PowerKids Press, 2010. Discover the amazing science at work during nuclear reactions and read about how reactors turn fuel into energy.

Websites

How Nuclear Power Works
http://science.howstuffworks.com/nuclear-power.htm
Take a tour through a nuclear reactor and learn more about the pros and cons of nuclear energy.

Student's Corner—Nuclear Reactors
http://www.nrc.gov/reading-rm/basic-ref/students/reactors.html
Just what is happening inside a nuclear reactor? Diagrams and descriptive text at this site take you step-by-step through the process.

A Student's Guide to Global Climate Change—Nuclear Energy
http://www.epa.gov/climatestudents/solutions/technologies/nuclear.html
At this US Environmental Protection Agency site, learn more about the role nuclear power plays in bringing power to the world.

LERNER

SOURCE

Expand learning beyond the printed book. Download free, complementary educational resources for this book from our website, www.lerneresource.com.

Index

Photo Acknowledgments

The images in this book are used with the permission of: © Mike_kiev/Dreamstime.com, p. 4;
© John R. Kreul/Independent Picture Service, p. 5; © snapgalleria/Shutterstock.com, p. 6; ESA/
NASA/SOHO, p. 7; © Monty Rakusen/Cultura/Getty Images, p. 8; © iStockphoto.com/hddigital, p. 9;
© iStockphoto.com/narvikk, p. 10; © Ralf Broskvar/Dreamstime.com, p. 11; Stefan-Xp/Wikimedia
Commons, p. 12; © iStockphoto.com/JohnCarnemolla, p. 13; © Bloomberg via Getty Images,
pp. 14, 16; © iStockphoto.com/malerapaso, p. 15; © Attila Kisbenedek/AFP/Getty Images, p. 17;
© iStockphoto.com/4X-image, p. 18; RUBEN SPRICH/REUTERS/Newscom, p. 19; Armin Weigel/dpa/
picture-alliance/Newscom; © Laura Westlund/Independent Picture Service, p. 21; © Steve Allen/
Stockbyte/Getty Images, p. 22; © Jvdwolf/Dreamstime.com, p. 23; © Sovfoto/Universal Images
Group/Getty Images, p. 24; AP Photo, p. 25; AP Photo/HO, p. 26; Jens Wolf/dpa/picture-alliance/
Newscom, p. 27; © iStockphoto.com/maomaotou , p. 28; © iStockphoto.com/bncc369, p. 29; US
Forest Service photo, p. 30; © iStockphoto.com/Symbiont, p. 31; © Alexis DUCLOS/Gamma-Rapho/
Getty Images, p. 32; © Robin Nelson/ZUMA Press/CORBIS, p. 33; SunPower Corporation/
Department of Energy/National Renewable Energy Laboratory, p. 34; Michael J. Okoniewski/
Iberdrola Renewables, Inc./Department of Energy/National Renewable Energy Laboratory, p. 35;
© iStockphoto.com/Akropot, p. 36; © Fineart1/Shutterstock.com, p. 37.
Front Cover: © Vaclav Volrab/Shutterstock.com.

Main body text set in Adrianna Regular 14/20
Typeface provided by Chank